La Fleur

La Fleur

JASMINE LEWIS

iUniverse

LA FLEUR

iUniverse books may be ordered through booksellers or by contacting:

iUniverse
1663 Liberty Drive
Bloomington, IN 47403
www.iuniverse.com
1-800-Authors (1-800-288-4677)

ISBN: 978-1-5320-0389-9 (sc)
ISBN: 978-1-5320-0390-5 (e)

Library of Congress Control Number: 2016913190

Print information available on the last page.

iUniverse rev. date: 09/19/2016

To Dominique A. Moss Hurst, I hope you enjoy this book!

Acknowledgments

I would like to thank God for giving me the gifts and experiences to write this book. I was sitting down with Him at the end of this book and realized something. All my heartaches I had experienced and all the times I'd cried and felt like jumping off the edge led me to write such a beautiful and powerful book. I have written sets and volumes of poetry in the past, and I have to say that I think *La Fleur* is the best one I have ever written. Thank You, Lord, for all You have allowed me to experience in order to write this book. I love You more and more each day.

I thank everyone who has bought this book. This book is truly from the heart, and I've put a lot of hard work into it. I hope to inspire as many people as possible with this book, and I hope that it will help many people with any feelings or emotions they have struggled with in life. One thing I would like is for Lady Gaga to find this book and sing one of my poems live onstage. It would make me feel wonderful and greatly accomplished to have someone as talented and beautiful as her use one of my poems as a song. She is a big inspiration to me and several other people. She is so energetic and enjoys what she does. I would like to thank her for inspiring me as well.

Finally, I save the best person for last. I would like to thank my older sister, Dominique Alexis Moss Hurst, for all her hard work in supporting me. She pushed me when no one else would and has been there for me at difficult times in my life when I wasn't sure I would ever make it through any of the obstacles I faced. She has been a guiding light to me and one of the leading inspirations in my life. She has taught me that love is more than just a fairy tale; it's also hard work and sacrifice. Thank you so much for sticking by me. I don't think I would have had the strength or courage to publish this book if it weren't for you. I love you so much! I hope you know there is no dream that is too big to accomplish as long as you have faith in God, who can work miracles lightning fast.

Thank you to the fans who purchase and read this book. There wouldn't be a me without any of you! Thank you, everyone!

La Fleur Opening

I wrote *La Fleur* at a time in my life when heartbreak was the most prominent. I have had a lot of hardships and difficulties in the realm of love. It's hard looking for love when you don't even know your value or who you are. When you're in love, it seems you will do anything for that special someone, including go against everything you stand for. I speak from experience when I say I almost lost myself this year. It took me a while to realize that I had to love myself first and have standards when it comes to dating and being in a relationship with anyone. Or else you will open up yourself to a world of hurt that you could have avoided.

La Fleur talks about the transition from an immature and inexperienced mind to a mature and experienced one. Sometimes a person does have to go through things, but I believe that some things can be avoided with proper knowledge, advice, and experience. Proper knowledge and experience isn't always given. That is why we are warned through the experiences of others at times. It is my greatest hope that everyone who reads this book will take a piece of my story, learn something new, and apply it to his or her life.

La Fleur

La fleur is very beautiful,
Full of radiant color and fragrance—
Full of life.
La fleur didn't get that way overnight.
It took some time before it became so beautiful and colorful.

La fleur needed two things to grow:
The sun and the rain.
The sun is bright and blinding.
It brings out all the birds and bees.

Smiles are worn, and laughter is shared at this time,
While the rain is very distraught, wet, gray, and gloomy.
Tears and heartbreaks are present,
But at this time, things grow,
Such as plants, animals, and people.

The rain signifies a time of badness but also change.
But when you place the sun and rain together,
You get a beautiful flower.
The sun dries up all the rain and pain.
Now la fleur is ready to blossom and shine.

Sea of Hearts

Hundreds of hearts are floating at sea,
Forever searching for the one true love—
Someone to find and hold them.
Some luck up to find their soul mates
While others are lost at sea, still searching.
How long will it take for a heart to find joy?

Some prefer solitude
While others desire love.
But love isn't for every heart?
All hearts respond to different things;
Therefore they must be treated differently.

One day a person will find herself floating in the sea of hearts.
What will she do?
People say that love can make the heart do strange things.
How?

They say love touches the heart in certain ways.
Will I ever experience these feelings if I ever fall into the sea of hearts?

No!
I shall never let my heart fall.
Nothing good can certainly come of it.
I must protect my heart from that dreadful sea.

No, I won't ever fall.
I don't want to be forever searching for the one.

No, I shall never fall.

I'm Slipping

My mind has a recollection of bad visions
Due to my bad decisions.
Oh, I'm slipping.
I feel it.
Oh, I'm sinning.
All the while I thought I was winning.

I caught a glimpse of a boy.
It seems I've fallen into a decoy.
It wasn't by choice—
I yielded to the sound of his voice.

Oh, how to escape this terrible noise!
The sound is hardly something to rejoice.

Oh, I forgot my mission.
I forgot to proceed with precision.
I've found myself slipping.

Oh, Lord, I think I'm sinning.
I'm not winning;
I'm losing.

My mind holds a recollection of bad visions
Due to bad decisions.
I slipped.
The devil made me feel it,
Out of my guilt,
Due to my bad decisions.

I forgot my mission.
I forgot to proceed with precision.

The Lonely Fool

It's just no one and you.
Oh, how you've become the lonely fool.
You were just a tool.
Look at him as he walks away, so cold and cool.
He freezes your heart—
How cruel!

It's just no one and you.
Oh, how you've become the lonely fool.
It seems no one wants you.

But it's true—
All the happiness lies within you.
Oh, this is true.

It's just no one and you.
As you feel you're about to lose,
Keep calm and cool.
It's the only way to go
Before you lose your soul—
Before you lose your soul.

Girl, hold your head up high.
Let that cruel man pass you by.
Life's too short to die,
To just feel sorry and cry.

Live your life.
You will survive.

There

There I lost my heart looking into your eyes.
I couldn't figure out why
Out spawned love.

I floated down this stream a time or two.
It was like I was going down it without a clue.
But that's how I found you.
I lost myself in you.

Baby, your heart drew me.
There I flew in your arms.
I forgot all those other flames.
There I saw a man with a heart.
There I was captured.

Carry me away,
Carry me away,
Because here with you is where I want to stay.

Behind Clothes

While holding hands, we share a groove that's close.
You took me to your room to show me who you are,
And we did go very far.

And behind faded and translucent clothes,
I got to know your soul.
Indeed we became one—
Flesh upon flesh.

I awoke to find myself in a wreck,
And just like that, you've left.
And so here begins the undesired effect.
I'm left alone to cry.
Oh, how sad it is when a fool cries!

And I thought he'd be by my side.
He came looking for a good time.
He came for a ride.

But he was supposed to be by my side.
How can I expect to survive
From making love to someone I've just met for the first time?

But love and affection were on my mind.
I gave it up,
And he just left within a night.

Oh, I don't dare be in denial!
Somehow it's not right.
Oh, how sad it is when a fool cries!
How sad it is when a fool cries.
I awoke to realize I made a mistake in one night.

Traveling Gypsy

She's longs for a home—
A place to belong—
So she roams,
Baby girl all alone.

Nobody wants her in his zone.
It all feels wrong,
But she's in a league all of her own.

Traveling gypsy, come with me.
Come and rest your feet.
Put your heart at ease.

"From the heartaches you've received
I'll put you at ease,"
Says the kind sir who rolls up his sleeves.

Traveling gypsy kindly winks
And waits to see the adventure waiting in the deep.
She takes the leap.

The kind sir catches her in his arms
And says, "No need to be alarmed;
I'll give you more than just superficial charm."

Traveling gypsy found her home.
Now she's no longer alone.
Like looking into her own soul,
Baby girl's in his zone—
Traveling gypsy no longer alone.

Thundering Footsteps

I can hear your thundering footsteps down the hall.
The sound of your voice calls.
The ambition in my heart falls
As I learn you're no longer in love.
You're racing to kill the dove.
It gets me in the blue
Because I don't think I can live without you.

You're rushing to hurt me.
In desperation I avoid thee.
It's foolish that I can't stand up to you.
I'm not that strong yet.

This is perhaps the hardest part—
The courage to follow through.

I fall short of myself.
Once I hear those thundering footsteps,
The clock strikes twelve.
And where is the love that once dwelt?

I gaze upon you from the top of the stairwell
And see the plan to keep you has failed.
Oh, it has failed!

I can hear your thundering footsteps down the hall.
The sound of your voice calls.
The ambition in my heart falls
As I learn you're no longer in love.
You're racing to kill the dove.
It gets me in the blue
Because I don't think I can live without you.

Thundering footsteps—
They've come to lead me to my death.
Oh, love, farewell!
Oh, love, farewell!

Thundering footsteps,
Don't you care?
Don't lead me to my death.

Thundering footsteps,
Thundering footsteps.

Reflection

I see you.
I try to touch the sun,
But I'm burned up before the task is done.
I'm always the slowest to run,
Always the last to know,
And, honey, it shows.

Your cruelty is reflected through your eyes,
And it's no surprise
That I try to hold it together and smile
Although my heart believes it's worthwhile.

It's worthwhile—
My heart believes it's worthwhile.

I try to love you,
But you push me aside.
The reflection of someone else is in your eyes.
Shall I cry?
Oh, lover, good-bye!
Oh, lover, good-bye!

Gypsy Lover

There you go again.
You've broken my heart, it seems,
And the reasons have come quite clear.
Your heart has gone away, my dear.
It seems your gypsy queen has called you away.
You leave me to find a path that is straight.
There she is, waiting for you by the gate.
You've cursed my name in hate.
You've gone to seal your fate.

Don't look back now—
Now that you look like the clown.
Don't you dare wear a frown.
Remember the way you kicked me while I was down?
The way you ran me to the ground
When you said with her true love was found?

Now you're back in town,
But I won't be around.
I am no longer bound.

Time is no longer between us,
And the love we've sown
Has faded to dust.

You don't feel it,
But this is the end of us.
Where's the trust?
The love we've known
Has been crushed.
This is the end of us.

Your gypsy queen
Seemed to be all you need.
Now it's done, and you grieve.
Farewell to your gypsy lover.

Now tell her that you love another.
She'll find it hard to recover.
Don't look back now—
Now that you've played the clown.
Wasn't it you who kicked me while I was down?
I am no longer bound.

Don't say you love me now.
It's too late;
You've sealed your fate.
It was more than you could take,
But I won't be the one to wait.
You've sealed your own fate.

But I won't be the one to wait.
Honey, it's too late.
I won't wait.

Farewell to you, my lover.
I'm taking time to recover.
Don't you dare hover—
Go be with your significant other.

Don't look back now.
Wasn't it you who kicked me while I was down?
My lover kicked me down!
He held me down to the ground.

Stagger

I stagger alone in a crowd.
I'm swayed by the noise in this town.
There you are standing around.
You're so cool, but I'm the clown.
I feel so lost without you.

So I reach for your hand.
You look at me and smile.
"Sorry I won't be around for a while"
Were the harsh words to come out of your mouth.

My hand is forced to let yours go.
I almost choke,
But this is a door that needs to be closed.
I try desperately gasping for air,
Knowing you won't be there.
It's all in good cheer.

I let you go, friend,
Like means to an end.
I let you go, friend.

I stagger alone in a crowd.
My heart is filled with gruesome sounds.
I'm alert now in this town.
Farewell, for I wish you well.
Those better days I'll be able to tell.
I reach for my goal ahead.

So I stagger alone in a crowd
To reach the other side.
I stagger alone in a crowd.

Gravity

No matter the chaos around us,
Gravity would lead me back to you.
You walked into my life.
Now I can't see it without you.
I would run away and try to forget you,
But the gravity would pull me back to you.

My eyes would behold this embrace.
It seems we've fallen so far from grace.
Still I long to see your face,
But at the expense of love, I suffer the cost.
My all gets lost,
And where are you now?

It feels so strange without you.
Now that I'm fine on my own,
You've come to pull me back.
I'm so confused.

I thought it was over between you and me.
It seems the gravity wants us near.
Hey, the gravity is what keeps us here.

No matter the trials,
No matter the chaos around us,
Gravity would lead us here,
Near and dear.

Darling, We Meet Again

Darling, we meet down this road again.
Those old feelings start to come back again
As I remember those special times.
There is a silver sparkle in your eyes.
Oh, how you long for the sunrise.
Remember when you were mine?
Oh, those were the times.

Hey, sunshine!
I've missed your smile.
Oh, it's been quite a while.
I didn't ever think you would come around.
I've seen a lot of faces around this town.

Hey, love, it's so good to see you come around.
Darling, we meet down this road again.
Those old feelings arise.
It's so nice to see you back in my life.

Midnight Darkness

In the darkness of the night,
I awake to find you not by my side—
But a letter to say good-bye.

The heart has capsized,
And the truth, I realized—
It was all lie.
It's all in the darkness of midnight.
The shadows begin to smile
And share laughter that of a child,
For their work is done now,
And no love is found.

Just Another Shot

I'll take another shot,
Just another ounce to add to the pain.
With each shot, the memory of you fades.
Oh, fool!

I'll be ashamed if you see me this way,
But I must forget the pain.
Oh, I'll be ashamed if you see me this way.

My heart is in a desperate state,
For I long to see your face,
But my vision is blurred,
And the memory of you fades away.

I reach out for you,
But you're not there.
You're not there.

So I'll take another shot.
It's all I've got—
Just another ounce to add to the pain.
I'll be waiting here.

I'll remain and pray you'll do the same,
But right now don't look—
I'm a mess.
Just another shot
To ease my broken heart.

Become One

You want us to become one
Under the sun.
No way, hun!

I don't want to regret it after it's all done.
No, I don't want to be the lonely one.
I hope you're not looking for fun
Because I can't be the lonely one.

You want us to become one
Under the moon.
Will that be my doom?
A flower needs lots of sun and rain to bloom.

Oh, baby, I really want to.
I really want you.
There are certain things you shouldn't do.
I can't be a fool.

You want us to become one
Under the sun.
Baby, are you the one?
I can't be the lonely one.

Baby, after it is all said and done,
Where do we run?
I can't be the lonely one.

Hot Summer Night

I feel the gentle summer's breeze
As I push through the crowd,
Keeping to myself and singing aloud
To the music playing in the streets.
People are singing and dancing.
Children are eating cotton candy.
And spinning around on that Ferris wheel.
Big lights and fireworks are everywhere.
I say to myself, "What a wonderful summer night."

Then steps out of the shadows
A pretty-eyed boy,
Blond-haired beauty with vanilla-like skin.
He glances at me and smiles.
My eyes say the same.

He asks me my name.
I reply with a laugh.
Sweet summer conversation begins.

I'm burning up.
I've got a 102 fever.
Trust me—it's not from the hot summer air;
It's from your gentle smile and stare.

So take me now
As we walk through the crowd,
Hand in hand,
Enjoying this hot summer night
With passion in our hearts.

We feel the gentle summer's breeze
As we push through the crowd,
Speaking sweet nothings to each other in the night,
Wondering why we met.
We aren't sure, but we know it's something beautiful.
We can tell.

So take me now
As we walk through the crowd.
We find love growing wild.

Yin and Yang

Yang
Formed in dust,
Built to love,
For you were made from the heavens above to be my love.
He breathed into you life.
Now He has given me you to love even through the strife.

For you were made for me,
Formed in dust,
Built to love,
Beautiful and pure—
Everything I want and need.
Of this I am sure.
Made in the Supreme One's image,
The counterpart to my very existence,
You will be with me from start to finish.

The man of my dreams I have envisioned,
A heart so pure and sweet lips to kiss,
Take my heart to a land of bliss.
This is my very wish.

Yin
Baby, I was made for you
So you would not be blue.
Come to me.
Let me be your sweet.
I've been through so much,
Losing myself in lust,
Longing for love's touch.
I want to feel love.

Open up;
Give yourself to me.
This is what I need—
My other half to be complete.
Baby, I was made from you
So you would not be blue.

Take me where I stand,
As I am—
Be my man.
My feelings within I know you understand.
Your heart beats the same rhythm as mine.
To me, you cannot lie.
God gave me to you for a wife.
Forever with me is where you will spend your life
Until the end of time.

Yin and Yang
Let us mingle together.
Let our spirits and flesh become one—
Yearning and burning desire.
When the time is right,
We will fall into passion when God commands,
For the day we came together,
We said it was forever.

Whether the sun shines or not,
Don't let our love spoil and rot.
Staying firm and firm,
Blocking out parasites and worms.
When we have lived, loved, and learned all we could,
Ashes and dust whence we came, and so shall we return.

Vanilla Sunrise

Skin so white and pure,
Piercing brown eyes,
A lovely, bright smile—
Make the sun rise and set on my heart.

Yea, be my vanilla sunrise.
Not sure if it is quite right.
My heart won't let me think that far,
Although my mind keeps saying, "Watch out!"
But I don't care.

The way he moves when he walks inside a room—
Such confidence,
Such appeal.
He turns to look at me.
I feel my heart racing.
Can't fight the urge to smile,
Although I've tried.
Can't fight the urge to smile.

He speaks, and there is such gentleness in his voice.
I can't speak back to him the way I want,
So I try to run away.
But love's gravitational pull reels me in.
Sucked into him completely,
I am trapped by his sweet, innocent smile.
I want to feel his soft skin wrapped around mine.

Tried to tell myself that you were just another pretty face,
But it was more than that.
Although I am not perfect,
You made me feel so.
Although I don't think myself to be beautiful,
You made me feel so.
Make the sun rise and set on my heart.

Yea, be my vanilla sunrise,
Always giving me a reason to smile.
Not quite sure if you're right for me.
My heart won't let me think that far,
Although my mind says be careful.
But I don't care.

Why don't you hold me?
Be my vanilla sunrise.
Make the sun rise and set on my heart.
Set my soul ablaze.
Make me yours,
My vanilla sunrise,
My vanilla sunrise,
My vanilla sunrise.
Kiss me.
Set my soul ablaze.
Make the sun rise and set on my heart.

Justified

I am not justified,
And I am not right.
I see the hurt in your eyes.
This is where I draw the line,
To say good-bye,
Gone on with life.
I'm left to the loneliness and strife.
We both have too much pride.
Neither of us wants to share our feelings inside.
The tension between us is there,
And with subtle stares,
Our words are in the air,
Left to those to twist and tear,
And you're unaware.

I know I was wrong to leave you this way.
I see it in the confusion on your face.
I won't be the first to say
I've done it a time or two,
Showcased my feelings to you.

But you won't do the same.
Secretive you remain.
You'll never admit it on your life—
This will start a fight.

Two wrongs don't make a right,
And I am not justified.
But I refuse to admit it tonight,
Not even with you in my sight,
For in my mind, I am justified,
Hanging on the edge of my pride.
You go your way, and I mine.

Desperation

The desperation's in my heart.
I need to hear your voice
On the other line.

The dial tone answers for the seventh time.
It's over.
I need to get this in my mind.

I tried to reach you,
To turn it around,
But you have no regard for how I feel now.

I've picked up the pieces of my broken heart
To turn over a new leaf for a new start.

Curtains Close

A voice says, "Turn back;
Remember your heart's vow,"
But the courage in my heart is down,
Saying, "I need just a little time
To build the strength inside."

But the dream is over now,
And I awake to find no answer at your door,
For you're now and no more.

So much I wanted to explore.
This is the final act—
I regret the courage I lacked.

I follow my hands to my head
As I lay in bed.

Journey of a Broken Heart

The journey of a broken heart
Is long and hard,
Scary and dark,
But carry your scars,
For they're a part of who you are.

There's life after love.
The pain has made you tough.
Don't give up.
One day you'll find it's enough—
Through it all you survived.

Open your eyes.
Take the breath of life.
Now stride.

Paths Crossed

It's been a while since our paths crossed,
For I thought you were a memory in my past,
But as I see you, the mind is emerged in flashbacks.

The heartache has died,
And the night has come.
It has cast its spell, and love has begun.
Now we feel forever young.

Come—there is much to be done
Just before the morning sun,
Before you're gone.
I need just this once.

Leave your skateboard at the door.
Place your clothes on the floor.
Give me a little more,
And with our bodies, we must explore
Our passion is deep.

As the room is filled with heat and heartbeats,
As we whisper promises to keep,
Promises in the dark,
This is where we're bound to start.
A new journey to embark—
It all starts with the closeness of hearts.

La Fleur Closing

Now you have learned what it takes to make a flower grow, the sun and the rain. Some people only wish for the sun and curse the rain. I've found myself here so many times, and I've always longed after the sun but always remained apprehensive of the rain. I'm a very optimistic person, and anyone like me has no time to grieve or be sad, but I learned to grieve and be sad a lot. At times I wasn't sure I was going to make it, but the Lord God made sure I was set up for success. I love Him for everything He allowed me to experience. I have truly grown in the realm of love. I am happy to see I have a more optimistic look on life and on love.

About the Author

My name is Jasmine K. Lewis, and I'm a writer from the state of Georgia. I have traveled around the United States. Writing has been a big part of my life ever since seventh grade. I grew up watching one of my older sisters, Kelli Monique Lewis Davis, write stories and poems in her free time, which inspired me to start writing my own. The first thing I wrote, "Vampire in the Night," was a short story about kids who have an encounter with a vampire after their parents leave the house. Since that time, I have written many stories and poems that I have made into collections, which I hope the world will read one day. Unfortunately I don't remember the first poem I wrote since I started off with writing stories first. Most of my poems and stories are written from experiences. I guess you could say that most of my poems and stories have pieces of me sprinkled on the page in an artistic way.

I have come to find that writing is an art in which I can express myself freely without boundaries. On several occasions, writing has helped me to relax and get my emotions out and deal with the things I have been feeling. I am in love with writing and don't think I could ever be without it.

So to those who are writers out there, my best advice to you is to keep writing and exploring emotions. Never be afraid to let the world hear your story through words. Someday you will capture the world's attention, so never give up.

Printed in the United States
By Bookmasters